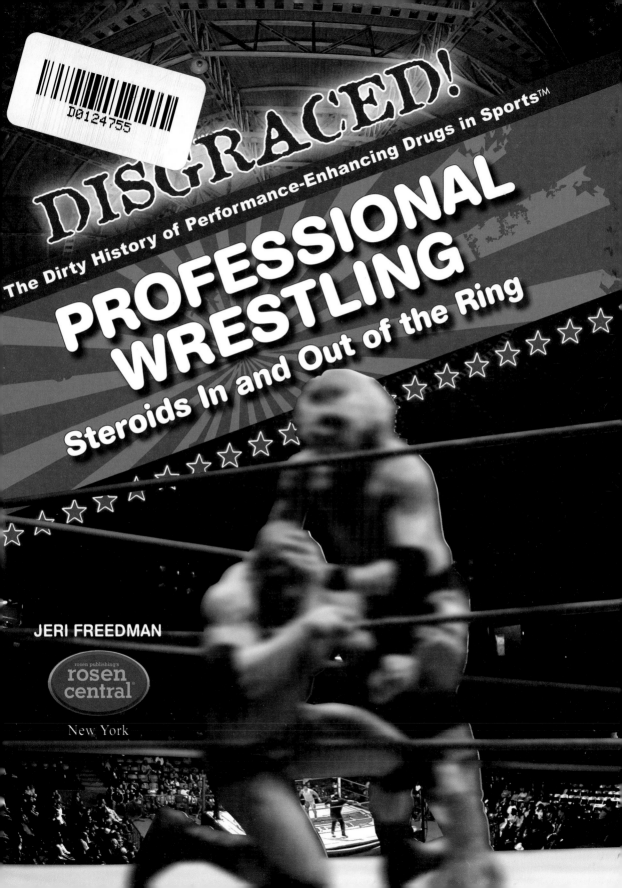

DISGRACED!

The Dirty History of Performance-Enhancing Drugs in Sports™

PROFESSIONAL WRESTLING

Steroids In and Out of the Ring

JERI FREEDMAN

rosen publishing's
rosen central®

New York

Published in 2010 by The Rosen Publishing Group, Inc.
29 East 21st Street, New York, NY 10010

Library of Congress Cataloging-in-Publication Data

Freedman, Jeri.
Professional wrestling: steroids in and out of the ring / Jeri Freedman.—1st ed.
    p. cm.—(Disgraced! the dirty history of performance-enhancing drugs in sports)
Includes bibliographical references and index.
ISBN-13: 978-1-4358-5305-8 (library binding)
1. Wrestling—Corrupt practices—United States—Juvenile literature.
2. Wrestlers—Drug use—United States—Juvenile literature. 3. Doping in sports—United States—Juvenile literature. I. Title.
GV1198.12.F74 2009
796.812—dc22

                                                                    2009001041

Manufactured in the United States of America

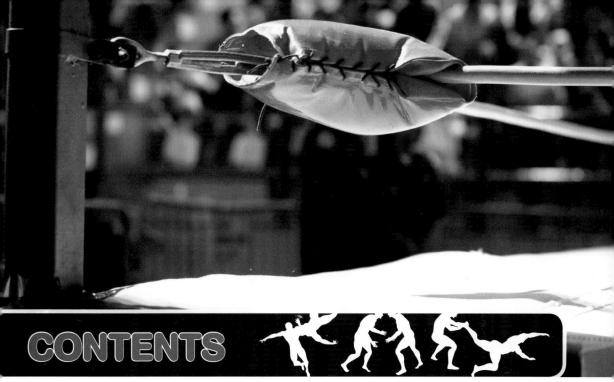

CONTENTS

Introduction

"Stackers." "Pumpers." "Gym candy." "Weight trainers." And, most commonly, "juice." These are all slang terms for steroids. Steroids are an all-too-common and dangerous part of the sports scene today. One sport that has been closely linked to steroid use is professional wrestling. In the 1990s and 2000s, numerous scandals involving steroid use by wrestlers were reported in the press. The concern over steroid use has led World Wrestling Entertainment (WWE), the largest wrestling promotion organization in the world, to start a program to discourage steroid use.

What are steroids? They are a type of hormone. Hormones are chemicals found in the body. They control body functions like the growth of tissue. The steroids abused most often are forms of the male sex hormone testosterone. Produced primarily in the testes, testosterone causes the development of such male characteristics as facial hair and large muscles. These testosterone-related hormones are called anabolic steroids, meaning they build up muscle. It is this aspect that makes them appealing to wrestlers, who are expected to look extremely large and muscular. It would take a lot of time and effort to build up the type of huge muscles that pro wrestlers are expected to have by exercise alone.

Wrestler Chris Benoit appears at a 2006 WWE match in Hershey, Pennsylvania. A former steroid user, Benoit was found dead on June 24, 2007.

But there are costs to wrestlers, their families, and society as a whole from the abuse of steroids. This book examines the use of steroids in pro wrestling and its negative effects on the wrestlers and the sport. It also explores the personalities involved and the scandals steroids have caused.

Chapter 1

Wrestling, Steroids, and Death

The March 2008 issue of *Sports Illustrated* features the article "The Godfather." In it, authors L. Jon Wertheim and David Epstein discuss the career of Tony Fitton. A former British powerlifter, Fitton claimed to have supplied steroids to high-profile athletes in the 1980s. Among his customers were "a good few in the WWF" (the World Wrestling Federation, which became today's WWE, or World Wrestling Entertainment). One of his clients was Randy Poffo, better known as Randy "Macho Man" Savage. Fitton said he didn't like Savage's stage persona, but the late John Minton (a.k.a. Big John Studd) told him that Savage was a good guy and that he should take on the rising star as a client. Savage declined to comment for the *Sports Illustrated* story, but the magazine reported that he has publicly admitted to trying steroids. The Macho Man retired in 2004 and, as of 2008, was still alive. However, not all steroid-using pro wrestlers are so fortunate.

The Biggest Downside of Steroid Use

Over the years, a number of wrestlers have died of physical problems that resulted from the long-term use of steroids. For example, on October 19, 2003, Mike Hegstrand, better known as the Road Warrior Hawk, died from an enlarged heart. In his book *Tribute II*, author Dave Meltzer notes that Hegstrand admitted to heavy steroid use during his wrestling career. When he died, Hegstrand was only forty-six years old.

On August 13, 2007, pro wrestling champion Brian "Crush" Adams collapsed and died in his home. He was only forty-four years old. Authorities found steroids in Adams's house.

Another highly publicized case involved Eddie Guerrero, who joined WWE in 2000. Guerrero died on November 13, 2005, at the age of thirty-eight. As reported on WrestlingInc.com, the autopsy report published by the Hennepin County medical examiner revealed that he died of heart disease. Specifically, the coroner said, Guerrero's heart was enlarged and showed a narrowing of the blood vessels that supplied it with blood and oxygen. The coroner did not name steroid use as the cause of death. But in interviews, Guerrero's wife blamed her husband's death on his use of steroids and other drugs, as well as his extreme workout regimen.

A third case involved Brian Adams, who had wrestled in the pro circuit until 2003 under the name "Crush." On August 13, 2007, Adams's wife found him at home, unconscious and not breathing. Paramedics were unable to revive him. According to a FOX News story published August 15, 2007, steroids were found in his house, suggesting that the drugs may have played a role in his death. Adams was only forty-four years old when he died.

Professional Wrestling's Steroid Problem

A March 2004 *USA Today* article by Jon Swartz points out that "despite some attempts to clean up an industry sold on size, stamina and theatrics, wrestlers die young at a staggering rate." For the article, *USA Today* reporters examined medical documents, autopsies, and police reports and interviewed wrestlers' families. They found that since 1997, at least sixty-five wrestlers age forty-five and younger had died. Twenty-five of them had died from heart problems, in many cases because of enlarged hearts. According to medical examiner Keith Pinckard, who was quoted in the *USA Today* article, "Wrestlers have death rates about seven times higher than the general U.S. population. They are 12 times more likely to die from heart disease than other Americans 25 to 44."

Why Is Steroid Abuse So Widespread in Wrestling?

Millions of dollars flow into pro wrestling. The executives who run organizations like WWE are exceptionally rich. And just like any other stars, top wrestlers can

Medical Uses of Steroids

Most anabolic steroids like testosterone are naturally produced in the testes. Some testosterone is produced by the adrenal glands (small glands that sit on the kidneys). A small amount of testosterone is also produced in women's ovaries because women need some testosterone for body processes, such as healthy bone growth.

Anabolic steroids are used to treat certain medical disorders. For example, they are prescribed for boys and men who don't produce enough male hormones for normal development. Typically, medical treatment with steroids is intended to increase the production of muscle, bone, or blood cells. In addition, steroids are used to treat some forms of the blood disease anemia and for osteoporosis, which is a loss of bone that often occurs as people age.

Using steroids when one doesn't have a medical condition that requires them can have serious health consequences. (See chapter 3.) One major problem with illegal steroids is that users generally take ten to sixty times the dosage prescribed for medical purposes. Such doses lead to abnormally large muscle development. Many wrestlers have relied on steroid use as a shortcut to building huge muscles and a larger-than-life physique.

make huge sums of money. The problem is that to be a celebrity in the field, one must appear abnormally large and muscular. Both the "good guys" and the "bad guys" look more like the superheroes and supervillains in comic books than real people. Moreover, the spectacular stunts that the athletes perform can take a

The Edge (Adam Copeland) in a 2008 Sydney, Australia, match. Despite pain and injury, wrestlers perform night after night. According to an August 30, 2007, article in *Sports Illustrated*, Copeland was known to have acquired steroids and human growth hormone from 2004 to 2007.

devastating toll on their bodies. To stay in the limelight, wrestlers must perform night after night, despite pain and injuries. These demands can cause wrestlers to turn to steroids, rather than risk a loss of income.

Many young men who become wrestlers have only a high school education. Wrestling offers them a once-in-a-lifetime chance to earn large sums of money and become a celebrity. The promise of money and fame often blinds them to the negative consequences of using performance-enhancing drugs. They don't see the potential for embarrassment and shame in being arrested for using illegal drugs. And they ignore the possibility that they will suffer from physical problems for the rest of their lives—and maybe even die a premature death.

Chapter 2

Performance-Enhancing Drugs in Wrestling

The history of performance-enhancing steroids can be traced back to scientific discoveries of the mid-nineteenth century. Arnold Berthold, a German scientist, is credited with some of the earliest findings regarding the development of male sexual characteristics. Around 1849, he transplanted the testes from roosters into the abdomens of other roosters, whose own had been removed. With the transplanted testes, the roosters developed normal male characteristics and behaviors. This demonstrated that there was some substance produced in the testes that controlled normal male development.

Much later, in 1931, another German scientist, Adolf Butenandt, first isolated a male steroid called androsterone. Then, in 1935, scientists isolated testosterone, a steroid even stronger than androsterone. Androsterone, testosterone, and other steroids quickly captured the interest of European pharmaceutical companies, which began looking for ways to manufacture and market the drugs.

Enhancing Performance

During the first few decades of the twentieth century, professional wrestling was a competitive sport like boxing and weightlifting. However, by the 1940s, promoters discovered that spectators were more interested in outlandish exploits than in wrestling as an athletic competition. Wrestling began to switch from being a sport to being a spectacle, featuring scripted performances with heroes and villains. In the 1940s to 1950s, characters like Gorgeous George (George Wagner) became celebrities, as popular as Hulk Hogan would be in the 1980s and 1990s. These performances were full of color and violence and larger-than-life, cartoon-ish characters. One way that the characters got to be larger than life was by using performance-enhancing drugs (PEDs).

Use of PEDs became a widespread problem in the years just after World War II. In the late 1930s and 1940s, a class of drugs called amphetamines was developed. These were stimulants, which are drugs that make people feel as though they have more energy. Athletes promptly started using them because they believed the drugs improved their performance, allowing them to run, lift weights, and train longer and harder before fatigue set in.

With athletes, including wrestlers, regularly using amphetamines to

Interest in physical fitness is not a recent phenomenon. As this 1885 photo shows, there has long been a fascination with men displaying strength and athletic skill.

improve their performance, it did not take long for steroids to make their mark on the sports scene as well. As word of the energizing and strength-enhancing effects of steroids spread, they became a drug of choice. In the beginning, steroid use was mostly confined to weightlifting, where there is an obvious advantage to having bigger, stronger muscles. Soviet weightlifters were the first to use steroids, in the 1950s. But by the 1960s, the drugs were being used by Olympic weightlifters from several countries, including the United States. Knowledge of steroids passed from weightlifters to other types of athletes who wanted a

"Gorgeous" George Wagner works the crowd at a 1949 match at Madison Square Garden in New York City. Gorgeous George was not known to have used steroids.

competitive edge. By the end of the 1960s, the use of steroids was common among professional athletes.

Laying the Groundwork

The history of modern wrestling began in the 1920s, when promoter Roderick James (Jess) McMahon had the idea of moving wrestling from the backstreets to a professional sporting venue. In partnership with boxing promoter Tex Rickard, McMahon had begun promoting boxing matches at Madison Square Garden in New York City. By the 1930s, McMahon had begun promoting wrestling events.

Steroids and the Ideal Body

In the twentieth century, two things influenced the use of steroids among certain athletes and fitness enthusiasts. First, anabolic steroids were legal until 1991 and readily available to the public. Second, people started becoming more health conscious, actively seeking ways to improve their vitality, strength, and general health.

As a result of these influences, a bodybuilding craze swept the United States, with men competing to see who could develop the most muscular body. A German man named Eugene Sandow started the bodybuilding movement. He began hosting competitions in which men displayed their muscles and competed in wrestling matches to demonstrate their strength. Sandow promoted the idea of an "ideal" body with perfect proportions. The public's interest in early bodybuilding competitions led to a slew of books with advice on how to improve one's body. The interest in bodybuilding also led to the rise of gymnasiums and health clubs. These, in turn, provided a place where men could wrestle to enhance and demonstrate their physical strength.

Around the same time, Joseph Raymond Mondt, Ed "Strangler" Lewis, and Billy Sandow formed a partnership. They promoted a new style of more exciting wrestling developed by Mondt, called "slam-bang western-style wrestling." Eventually, the partnership dissolved. In the early 1950s, Mondt joined forces with Vincent J. McMahon, Jess McMahon's son, to create the Capitol Wrestling Corporation (CWC).

At the 1912 Olympics in Stockholm, Sweden, Martin Klein (*right*) of Russia competes with Alfred Asikainen of Finland in Greco-Roman wrestling. Today's pro wrestling has little in common with the wrestling seen here.

But the relationship between wrestling and the media changed that. Although wrestling had started to move into the mainstream, it still remained a minor sport with a modest following. Then, in 1963, Vincent J. McMahon replaced his father, Jess, at the reins of the CWC. Shortly thereafter, Vince converted the CWC into the World Wide Wrestling Federation (WWWF). In 1979, McMahon changed the name to the World Wrestling Federation (WWF). Then, in 1980, Vincent K. McMahon, Vincent J. McMahon's son, formed Titan Sports. In 1982 he bought his father's company. Vincent J. McMahon became the mastermind behind the modern professional wrestling spectacle that we know today.

WWE chairman Vince McMahon has been the driving force behind the growing popularity of wrestling in the late twentieth century. In 1989, he admitted to taking steroids when they were still legal for personal use.

The Rise of Wrestling and the Media

McMahon hired Hulk Hogan (Terry Gene Bollea), who had starred in *Rocky III* in 1982. Using the popular star wrestler to great advantage, McMahon began selling television rights to WWF events and producing videotapes of the matches. His approach was a radical change from the traditional promotion of wrestling matches, which typically had different companies presenting the events in different parts of the country. McMahon made a great deal of money from his television contracts, advertising revenue, and videotape sales. He used that money to hire the best, most entertaining talent available, creating bigger and more exciting matches as he went along. In 1983, McMahon started taking advantage of cable television to present wrestling events that caught the attention of an ever-growing audience.

McMahon's approach was to turn wrestling into mass entertainment. He wanted to get mainstream viewers to watch his shows. In 1985, he furthered this goal by creating *WrestleMania*. Viewers tuned in to see colorful heroes and villains engage in dramas that went far beyond two strong men grappling. The demand for scripted shows featuring gimmicky characters led to ever more exotic events, such as *Extreme Championship Wrestling*.

In 2002, the WWF dropped "Federation" from its name and became World Wrestling Entertainment (WWE). McMahon's WWE was making vast sums of money from televised matches. It also reaped millions from tie-in products, including action figures, computer games, and other branded merchandise. Wrestling had become big business. Everyone wanted a piece of the action, and nobody wanted to ruin a good thing. However, scandals involving the abuse of performance-enhancing drugs soon took center stage.

Chapter 3

Attempts to Control Steroid Abuse

I n 1990, the U.S. Congress passed a revision, or updated version, of the Controlled Substances Act. The goal of this piece of legislation is to control the manufacture, distribution, and sale of drugs that are deemed potentially harmful, are a danger to public health, or are likely to be abused. By the time the Controlled Substances Act was passed, there was growing concern about the negative health effects of steroids, as well as the unfair advantage they gave to the athletes who used them.

Congress first added steroids to the Controlled Substances Act in 1991. The Anabolic Steroid Control Act, first passed in 1990, was updated in 2004. This law added more steroids to the list of controlled substances and increased the power of the U.S. Drug Enforcement Administration (DEA) to fight the illegal production, sale, and distribution of steroids. Under the Anabolic Steroid Control Act of 2004, possession of illegal steroids is punishable by up to one year in jail for a first offense and up to two years if a person has been previously convicted.

Illegal Steroid Production and Distribution

The body naturally produces steroids in tiny quantities. However, widespread distribution of anabolic steroids is possible because synthetic (man-made) forms of these chemicals can be manufactured. Unlike natural steroids, synthetic

OUR OFFICE IS CLOSED UNTIL FURTHER NOTICE AND DR. ASTIN CANNOT BE REACHED FOR COMMENTS.

In June 2007, federal drug agents raided the office of Dr. Phil Astin, wrestler Chris Benoit's personal physician. The agents were searching for the doctor's records, as well as other items, named in their search warrant.

steroids can be produced in large quantities. Some illegal steroids are obtained from crooked pharmacists, doctors, or veterinarians who sell commercial medical steroids to people who don't need them for medical problems. However, most illegal steroids come from one of two sources. First, much of the steroids sold illegally are imported from legitimate pharmaceutical and chemical companies abroad. (Steroids are legal in certain Eastern European countries, for example.) A second source, much closer to home, is the network of secret laboratories in the United States and Canada that produces the steroids for sale on the street.

World Wrestling Entertainment Crackdown

The first pro wrestling steroid testing program was begun in July 1991. However, that program was notorious for being ineffective and too lax on those caught using the drugs.

More recently, in February 2006, World Wrestling Entertainment, Inc., the largest wrestling promotion organization in the world, implemented the WWE Talent Wellness Program. This program is designed to discourage the use of performance-enhancing drugs, including steroids. The program combines extensive drug testing with medical testing to evaluate each wrestler's heart and blood pressure. According to the policy, if a wrestler has health issues, appropriate treatment will be arranged.

WWE's substance abuse policy outlaws the nonmedical use of PEDs. It also prohibits the distribution of such drugs. In the program, any wrestler can be tested randomly. Wrestlers are given an initial test, without penalty, to see where they stand. If an individual fails his or her next test, he or she will be suspended for thirty days. A second positive test will result in a sixty-day suspension, or until treatment at an in-patient substance abuse treatment facility is completed. Failing a third test will result in the termination of the wrestler's contract.

Breaking the Silence on Steroid Use in Wrestling

By the early 1990s, government authorities were sharpening their focus on the abuse of anabolic steroids in high-profile sports. It wasn't long before professional wrestling came into their crosshairs. The first to fall was Dr. George T. Zahorian III, a physician from Harrisburg, Pennsylvania. In June 1991, he was convicted on eleven counts of illegally distributing anabolic steroids and other PEDs. Before he started supplying a number of WWF wrestlers with steroids, Zahorian had worked as a state-appointed ringside physician at professional wrestling events in Pennsylvania. His arrest focused national attention on steroid abuse in wrestling.

According to the November 1991 edition of *FDA Consumer*, when authorities searched Zahorian's papers, they discovered receipts for Federal Express shipments of steroids and other controlled substances to professional wrestlers. Among them were Richard Vigneault, also known as Rick Martel, and Rowdy Roddy Piper, whose real name is Roderick Toombs. Martel appeared with the World Wrestling Federation, the American Wrestling Association, and World Championship Wrestling from 1982 to 1998. Piper appeared with several major wrestling organizations, including the WWF, from 1984 to 1996, and more recently with WWE, in the mid-2000s.

Three other wrestlers besides Martel and Piper appeared at Zahorian's trial, testifying that they had bought steroids from the physician. These included Brian Blair, Dan Spivey, and onetime WWE champion and wrestling great Eldridge Wayne Coleman, who wrestled under the stage name "Superstar Billy Graham." A year later, while appearing on *The Phil Donahue Show*, Coleman again admitted to regularly using steroids. Active in wrestling in the 1970s and 1980s, Coleman retired in 1988 because of health problems related to steroid use, including problems with his hips and ankles. He also required a liver transplant in 2002. After his retirement, Coleman began giving talks to high school students about the dangers of steroid use.

Getting Around the Law

Because of the legal risks, many of those in sports who use steroids—including wrestlers—try to obtain them from safer sources, such as crooked doctors.

Canadian WWE Hall of Fame wrestler Rowdy Roddy Piper was one of several wrestlers who testified at the trial of George Zahorian III regarding the doctor's sale of steroids to wrestlers. Piper is seen here in his trademark Scottish kilt.

Another approach is to obtain a legal prescription for steroids. Steroids can be prescribed legally to men who have abnormally low levels of testosterone. It is possible to give the false impression that a man suffers from this problem. One side effect of steroid use is that the body shuts down its natural production of steroids once it senses that it already has more steroids than it needs. Therefore, a man may take a large amount of steroids until his body stops making its own. Then, he stops taking steroids. Once the steroid level in his body has dropped, he goes to a doctor for a test. When the test comes back, it shows too little testosterone in the body and the doctor gives him a legal prescription for steroids because he or she thinks the patient has too little testosterone.

Chapter 4

The Effects of Steroid Abuse

In order to develop abnormally large muscles, people who use anabolic steroids generally take many times the dose given for medical purposes. Taking a huge amount of a substance like steroids is called megadosing. The massive increase in the level of steroids in the body causes an increase in all of the activities in the body controlled by anabolic steroids. This can have serious, negative effects on a person's physical and mental health. This chapter looks at such effects.

Physical Effects of Steroid Abuse

Steroids affect the cardiovascular system—in other words, the heart and blood vessels. The drugs can cause an increase in the force that is required for the heart to pump blood through the blood vessels. This is referred to as high blood pressure, or hypertension. High blood pressure can damage blood vessels.

Steroids also increase the low-density lipoprotein (LDL) cholesterol that the body produces. Cholesterol is a fatty substance that can clog arteries, making it more difficult for blood to get through. Clogged arteries increase a person's chances of suffering heart attacks and strokes. Heart attacks occur when blood cannot get through an artery to reach heart muscle, and strokes occur when blood cannot get through a blood vessel to reach the brain. In both cases, an organ deprived of blood can be damaged seriously, and death may occur. An unusually large number of wrestlers have died young of heart attacks, among them Michael "Jerry" Tuite ("The Wall," age thirty-five), Ray Traylor ("Big Boss

Ronnie Coleman won the Mr. Olympia title from 1998 to 2006. The pursuit of a body like Coleman's drives some to use steroids.

Man," age forty-one), and Ted Petty ("Rocco Rock," age forty-nine).

According to *USA Today*, Davey Boy Smith, whose stage name was "The British Bulldog," died at age thirty-nine in 2002 in Canada of an enlarged heart. A coroner's report found evidence of microscopic scar tissue, possibly from steroid abuse. Louis "Spicolli" Mucciolo was another wrestler who died of coronary (heart) disease. A 2007 FOXNews.com article said the autopsy report on Mucciolo indicated that investigators found an empty vial of testosterone, as well as pain pills and an anxiety-reducing drug. The Los Angeles County coroner's office determined the drugs might have contributed to Mucciolo's condition.

Abusing steroids can damage the liver, an organ that plays a vital role in purifying the blood by removing dead cells and toxins from the body. When the liver doesn't function properly, a person can get very sick. If it stops functioning altogether, a person can die. Steroid use has been linked to an increased risk of liver cancer. And the drugs may damage the kidneys, which play a key role in removing waste products from the body.

In addition to internal damage, steroid abuse affects the way that a person looks. It is common for people taking large amounts of steroids to develop acne and striae, or stretch marks. Gender-related changes are common, too, in people who abuse steroids. When a person takes steroids, the body recognizes that it has enough testosterone and doesn't need to make more. Therefore, men who use steroids may experience a reduction in sperm produced, difficulty getting an erection, and shrinking of the testes. Men's breasts may also grow because their body starts to put out more of the female hormone estrogen in an attempt to balance the amount of testosterone in their blood.

Women Wrestlers and Steroids

Women who take steroids get bigger muscles, but they also develop male physical characteristics—a process called masculinization. A woman's voice may deepen as her vocal cords thicken, her breasts may shrink, and she may start to grow facial hair. The high level of male sex hormones in her blood may cause her period to become irregular or stop altogether.

Female bodybuilders pose at the World Games of 2005 in Duisburg, Germany.

During the 1980s the World Wrestling Federation sponsored women's wrestling as well as men's. Currently, women wrestlers appear as counterparts to male wrestlers in the WWE's regular events. Steroid use doesn't just affect female pro wrestlers. In 2004, female Puerto Rican wrestler Mabel Fonseca was expelled from the Olympics when she tested positive for the steroid Stanozolol in a drug test.

Psychological Effects of Steroid Abuse

When a substance affects the mind, the effect is said to be psychological. Steroids can change a person's mood and behavior. They affect a part of the brain called the hypothalamus, which regulates mood, among other things. Testosterone stimulates the part of the brain that is responsible for aggression. People who use steroids often experience mood swings. They may go from being agitated and excited to being depressed (abnormally sad). In some cases, excessive steroid use can lead to feelings of anger that, in turn, can lead to violence.

Addiction to Steroids

The body contains chemical sensors that tell the brain when the level of a steroid in the body becomes too high or too low. The brain responds by sending a signal to the gland that is responsible for producing the hormone, telling it to make more or less. When a person overloads his or her system with steroids, chemical sensors tell the brain that the body has more of those steroids than necessary. In response, the body stops producing them. From that point on, the person must keep taking the steroids because the body no longer makes them. If the person stops taking the steroids, he or she will experience withdrawal symptoms, which may include weakness, fatigue, and serious depression.

Effects of Steroid Abuse Outside the Ring: The Case of Chris Benoit

Steroid abuse can increase aggression and violent behavior, affecting the way that abusers interact with others. They may pick fights. They may engage in

WWE wrestler Santino Marella has an angry confrontation with TV personality Jimmy Kimmel in 2003. While being angry inside the ring is a wrestler's job, those that take steroids might not be able to control their anger outside the ring.

domestic violence against their spouses and children. They may experience fits of violent anger commonly known as "'roid rage." One of the most notorious cases of a wrestler committing violence involved championship wrestler Chris Benoit.

On June 25, 2007, Benoit, his wife, and his son were found dead in their Georgia home. Authorities ultimately concluded that Benoit had killed his family and then committed suicide. While it may not be the only factor, evidence suggested that steroid use played a role in the crime. According to WSB-TV, Benoit's wife, Nancy, had expressed concern about her husband's use of steroids and threw them out. Eight months after the murder, the Fayette County, Georgia, staff's office released its report on the investigation.

Steroids may have been a factor in the tragic death of WWE superstar Chris Benoit and his wife and son.

As revealed in the *Atlanta Journal-Constitution*, the police report stated that Chris and Nancy Benoit were having marriage problems. Nancy was angry over her husband's use of steroids, and she was afraid of the effect that they were having on him. In addition, diary entries indicate that Chris Benoit was depressed. The police found steroids in the house, but a blood test revealed that the level in Benoit's blood was in the expected range for medical treatment. Because of his past steroid use, Benoit needed to take steroids to replace those that his body no longer made. Benoit's father claimed that Chris had mental problems as a result of repeated concussions in the course of his career.

It seems likely that multiple factors played a role in the Benoit tragedy. But the fact remains that either steroid use or withdrawing from such use may have contributed to the decline in his mental state, which led to the deaths.

Chapter 5

Scandals and Ruined Careers

The 1991 trial of Dr. George Zahorian III and the statements made by wrestler Eldridge Wayne Coleman (Superstar Billy Graham) about steroid use in wresting led to revelations of steroid use by other wrestlers. Since that time, a series of steroid-related scandals has rocked the wrestling world. This chapter examines some of these.

Hulk Hogan

David Shults, who wrestled under the name "Dr. D," came forward shortly after Coleman's revelations about steroid use. According to Irvin Muchnick's book, *Wrestling Babylon*, Shults admitted to using steroids. But he caused a far greater scandal by saying that Hulk Hogan used steroids as well. In fact, Shultz claimed to have personally injected Hogan with steroids "well over one hundred times."

Hogan is one of the most famous wrestlers in modern times. He won multiple world championships on the World Championship Wrestling, World Wrestling Federation, and World Wrestling Entertainment circuits. He is a member of the Wrestling Hall of Fame. Most recently, he co-hosted the television show *American Gladiators*. For some time after revelations about steroid abuse in wrestling began to appear, Hogan denied using the drugs. However, he was offered immunity (protection from prosecution) to testify at the July 1994 trial of Vincent K. McMahon. The wrestling promoter was on trial for allegedly

Wrestler Hulk Hogan, a celebrity both in and out of the ring, has confessed to using steroids. According to Hogan, he believed that his steroid use was legal.

conspiring to provide steroids illegally to members of his World Wrestling Federation (today's WWE).

According to an article in the July 15, 1994, edition of the *New York Times*, Hogan admitted during the trial that he had used steroids over the course of nearly fourteen years, obtaining them from Zahorian. Said the wrestler, "I believed it was legal because I had a prescription for it." Hogan also said that McMahon never "ordered" him to take steroids and never purchased any steroids for him. In the end, McMahon was acquitted of all charges. Nonetheless, the trial tarnished Hogan's legacy and, in the minds of many, cast suspicion on the entire WWF organization.

In spite of the federal trial against McMahon, or perhaps because of it, steroid use continued in professional wrestling. According to a March 12, 2004, *USA Today* article by Jon Swartz, fifteen current and former wrestlers interviewed by *USA Today* said they had used anabolic steroids both to develop and maintain an appropriate "look" and to be able to perform four to five nights, even when injured. In addition, some admitted to using human growth hormone (HGH), which is a strong muscle-building compound.

Others said they also used recreational drugs. Among those interviewed were Rowdy Roddy Piper and Scott Levy (Raven). Regarding the use of steroids, Levy said, "It's part of the job. If you want to be a wrestler, you have to be a big guy, and you have to perform in pain. If you choose to do neither, pick another profession."

More Scandals

A September 7, 2007, Associated Press article revealed that eleven professional wrestlers were linked to a nationwide investigation of illegal steroid sales. Among the wrestlers being investigated was Randy Orton. Allegedly, he obtained prescriptions for six drugs, including steroids, in the spring and summer of 2004 from two of the doctors being investigated.

Another wrestler who appeared in the news because of steroid use is Charlie Haas of the WWE. In an August 30, 2007, article in *Sports Illustrated*, Haas was named as one of several wrestlers who purchased illegal steroids.

Charlie Haas dominates at the 2006 WWE RAW Summerslam event in Sydney, Australia. He now promotes nutrition as an alternative to steroid use.

Haas bought them between August 2006 and January 2007. However, he maintained that he thought his purchases were legal and that he was taking the drugs to combat pain related to knee reconstruction surgery. In a November 29, 2008, *SLAM! Wrestling* article by Tim Baines, Haas was quoted as saying, "I got caught up in it. I thought I was doing something legal. I'd had both my knees reconstructed. I was doing it for maintenance. I'm not going to lie about it. I'm not proud of what I did, and I have to live with it. It was wrong, a mistake that I made. I thought I was doing something to surpass the pain. But what I was doing was hurting myself. And it was embarrassing to my family and to the company. Since then, I've really gotten into sports nutrition ... Kids have to realize if you're weaker or smaller, they shouldn't take steroids to get stronger and bigger. Just eat right. It can be done right."

In August 2007, an ongoing investigation into steroid trafficking by the Albany, New York, district attorney's office revealed that steroids were being supplied illegally to WWE wrestlers by Signature Pharmacy in Orlando, Florida. The *New York Daily News* reported that WWE planned to suspend ten wrestlers in connection with the probe. WWE refused to release the names of those who would be suspended, but the *Daily News* listed the following wrestlers as having received drugs from the pharmacy: Randy Orton, Charles Haas Jr., Adam Copeland (The Edge), Robert Huffman (Booker T), Shane Helms, Mike Bucci, Anthony Carelli, John Hennigan (Johnny Nitro), Darren Matthews (William Regal), Ken Anderson (Mr. Kennedy), Eddie Fatu (Umaga), Shoichi Funaki, and Chavo Guerrero.

WWE Raw wrestler Randy Orton allegedly received steroids from a pharmacy that was under investigation as part of a nationwide law operation.

According to the *Wrestling Observer Newsletter*, reported by Ryan Clark on WrestlingInc.com, Chavo Guerrero, an ECW champion, actually has two WWE suspensions. He was suspended for thirty days in 2006 under the WWE Wellness program. He was suspended for a second time in 2007 for sixty days, following a second steroid violation. On August 13, 2006, Randy Orton was suspended from house shows for a little over a month. To avoid embarrassment, Orton said he was taking a break to move into a new home. WWE suspensions mean that wrestlers are deprived of pay and their pay-per-view bonus. Also, those suspended are pulled from all non-televised house shows.

Steroid Use in High School and College Wrestling

Steroid use among young people in high school and college sports has become an area of major concern. With celebrity and the possibility of earning huge salaries dangling in front of young athletes, winning at all costs has become a major priority for many. Steroid use is a particular concern in sports where being large and strong gives one a competitive edge. Thus, athletes competing in football, boxing, and wrestling are prime targets for those who sell steroids. Sources of steroids include people who sell them at sporting events and teammates who are already taking them.

Concern over the problem is illustrated by a recent statement of policy by the National Athletic Trainers' Association (NATA). In addition to supporting a ban on all performance-enhancing drugs, the NATA statement says that "the long-term, irreversible, negative effects of banned substances on a young athlete's growing body are a frightening repercussion not worthy of improved athletic performance. While a broad ban on such substances is a start, an equally important weapon in the battle against steroid use is more thorough education of our athletes and parents."

Standing Up to Pressure

If you engage in high school or college wrestling, you may someday encounter a person who encourages you to use steroids. It can be difficult to stand up to pressure, especially if the person pressuring you is a teammate. And it is easy to fall into the trap of behaving like other people because you want to be accepted and feel connected. It's also easy to be persuaded that the only way you will succeed is if you use performance-enhancing drugs. Be aware of three facts:

- Unlike professional wrestling, where the participants' appearance is the key draw for audiences, high school and college wrestling are legitimate sports in which grappling skill and technique, not just absurdly giant muscles, are important.

College wrestling is about sport, not show. Taking steroids can result in your being banned from competition and damaging your body so that you can't compete in the future.

- Taking steroids increases your chances of having problems with your bones as well as your heart, liver, kidneys, and sexual organs. Steroids make it more likely that you will suffer an injury that affects your ability to play in the future.

- School, health care, and sports officials all have monitoring programs designed to detect steroid use by students. The police monitor steroid-selling Web sites and chat rooms. When they catch a student selling steroids, they often obtain the names of other students who have purchased them.

Using steroids is not only dangerous but could also end your school career and your future professional career. Even though it is difficult to stand up to peer pressure to use steroids, it is important to do so.

The Future

Recently, there has been widespread outrage among members of the media, Congress, parents, educators, and others about the effects of steroid abuse in professional sports. Much of this outrage stems from the influence that professional athletes have on impressionable youngsters. When young people come to believe that the use of steroids is acceptable in sports, they may be more likely to use them, too. Because of such concerns, existing drug testing and education programs have been expanded in many sports, including wrestling. Even more rigorous drug testing programs and tougher penalties are likely to be put in place in the near future. However, as long as there is fame and fortune to be had, eliminating the use of steroids in professional wrestling may be a long and difficult process.

GLOSSARY

adrenal glands Two small glands that sit on the kidneys.

amphetamine A drug that acts as a stimulant, making people feel "pepped up."

anabolic Building up; anabolic steroids build up muscle tissue.

anemia The condition of having too few red blood cells.

coroner Medical examiner; the person responsible for determining the cause of a person's death.

depressed Abnormally sad.

deprived Denied.

hormone Chemical produced in the body that regulates a body function, such as growth.

house show A non-televised wrestling event.

hypothalamus The part of the brain that, among other things, controls mood.

immunity In legal terms, protection from prosecution.

low-density lipoprotein (LDL) cholesterol "Bad cholesterol," which clogs blood vessels.

osteoporosis A condition characterized by bone loss, which often occurs as people age.

physique The size and shape of one's body.

prohibit To forbid or outlaw.

promoter In wrestling, a person who arranges matches.

protein The basic building block of tissue.

psychological Mental; having to do with the mind.

synthetic Artificial; man-made.

testosterone The hormone responsible for the development of male characteristics, such as facial hair and large muscles.

toxin A harmful or poisonous substance.

vitality The feeling of being energized and healthy.

FOR MORE INFORMATION

Canadian Centre on Substance Abuse
75 Albert Street, Suite 300
Ottawa, ON K1P 5E7
Canada
(613) 235-4048
Web site: http://www.ccsa.ca
This organization provides a variety of reports and reference materials on
    substance abuse in Canada.

Drug Policy Information Clearinghouse
P.O. Box 6000
Rockville, MD 20849-6000
(800) 666-4332
Web site: http://www.whitehousedrugpolicy.org
This organization provides a wide range of information on drugs, drug abuse
    treatment and prevention, and law enforcement, as well as publications.

National Drug Intelligence Center
319 Washington Street, 5th Floor
Johnstown, PA 15901-1622
(814) 532-4690
Web site: http://www.usdoj.gov/ndic
A division of the U.S. Department of Justice, this organization provides online and
    printed publications about popular illegal drugs, including steroids.

National Institute on Drug Abuse
National Institutes of Health
6001 Executive Boulevard, Room 5213
Bethesda, MD 20892-9561

(301) 443-1124

Web site: http://www.drugabuse.gov

This organization provides a wealth of information on drug abuse of all types, including steroids, and offers a variety of publications for students and adults.

Substance Abuse and Mental Health Services Administration

1 Choke Cherry Road, Room 8-1036

Rockville, MD 20857

(800) 273-8255

Web site: http://www.samhsa.gov

This agency provides resources to help people recover from substance abuse problems.

World Wrestling Entertainment

1241 East Main Street

Stamford, CT 06902

(203) 352-8600

Web site: http://www.wwe.com

In addition to the latest news on wrestling, this organization provides a newsletter that you can sign up for.

Web Sites

Due to the changing nature of Internet links, Rosen Publishing has developed an online list of Web sites related to the subject of this book. This site is updated regularly. Please use this link to access the list:

http://www.rosenlinks.com/dis/wres

FOR FURTHER READING

Aretha, David. *Steroids and Other Performance-Enhancing Drugs*. Berkeley Heights, NJ: Enslow, 2005.

Egendorf, Laura K. *At Issue: Drugs and Sports*. Chicago, IL: Greenhaven, 2005.

Fitzhugh, Karla. *Health Issues: Steroids*. Chicago, IL: Raintree, 2003.

Freedman, Jeri. *Drug Abuse and Society: Steroids*. New York, NY: Rosen Publishing, 2008.

Levert, Suzanne. *The Truth About Steroids*. New York, NY: Benchmark Books, 2004.

Lukas, Scott E. *The Drug Library: Steroids*. Berkeley Heights, NJ: Enslow, 2001.

Mintzer, Richard. *Steroids = Busted!* Berkeley Heights, NJ: Enslow, 2006.

Monroe, Judy. *Steroids, Sports, and Body Image: The Risks of Performance-Enhancing Drugs*. Berkeley Heights, NJ: Enslow, 2004.

Shields, Brian. *The Main Event: The WWE in the Raging '80s*. Stamford, CT: WWE Press, 2006.

Solomon, Brian. *WWE Legends*. Stamford, CT: WWE Press, 2006.

Walker, Ida. *Steroids: Pumped Up and Dangerous*. Broomall, PA: Mason Crest, 2007.

Baines, Tim. "Impersonations Paying Off for Haas." *Slam! Wrestling*, November 29, 2008. Retrieved February, 2009 (http://slam.canoe.ca/Slam/Wrestling/2008/11/28/7570381.html).

Clark, Ryan. "Eddie Guerrero's Cause of Death Officially Revealed." WrestlingInc.com, December 08, 2005. Retrieved January 7, 2009 (http://www.wrestlinginc.com/news/2005/128/eddie_guerrero_2266.shtml).

Clark, Ryan. "Stacy Comments on WWE/Steroids, FBI, Snitsky Pulled, Angle, & More." eWrestlingNews.com, October 23, 2008. Retrieved December 21, 2008 (http://www.ewrestlingnews.com/stories/Stacy_Comments_On_WWESteroids_FBI_Snitsky_Pul.shtml).

ESPN.com. "Female Wrestler Also Expelled." August 28, 2004. Retrieved December 21, 2008 (http://sports.espn.go.com/oly/summer04/gen/news/story?id=1869749).

ESPN.com. "Orton, Other Wrestlers Linked to Probe of Pharmacy." September 7, 2007. Retrieved November 20, 2008 (http://sports.espn.go.com/espn/news/story?id=2805155).

eWrestlingNews.com. "Haas Finally Comments on Past Steroid Use, Ortiz Note, RAW, SD!, More." November 29, 2008. Retrieved November 30, 2008 (http://www.ewrestlingnews.com/stories/Haas_Finally_Comments_On_Past_Steroid_Use_Ort.shtml).

FOX News. "Former Pro Wrestling Champion Brian 'Crush' Adams Died Monday After He Was Found Unconscious in His Home. He Was 44." August 13, 2007. Retrieved November 15, 2008 (http://www.foxnews.com/story/0,2933,293152,00.html).

FOX News. "Fox Facts: Famous Wrestling Deaths." June 26, 2007. Retrieved February, 2009 (http://www.foxnews.com/story/0,2933,286774,00.html).

Jendrick, Nathan. *Dunks, Doubles, Doping: How Steroids Are Killing American Athletics*. Guilford, CT: The Lyons Press, 2006.

Llosa, Louis Fernando, and L. Jon Wertheim. "Fourteen Wrestlers Tied to
    Pipeline." SportsIllustrated.com, August 30, 2007. Retrieved March, 2009
    (http://sportsillustrated.cnn.com/2007/more/08/30/wrestlers).

Lyons, Brendan J. "Steroids Beyond Sports." *Albany Times Union*, January 13,
    2008. Retrieved January 14, 2008 (http://timesunion.com/ASPStories/
    storyPrint.asp?StoryID=654817).

Meltzer, David. *Tribute II: Remembering More of the World's Greatest Wrestlers.*
    Champaign, IL: Sports Publishing LLC, 2004.

Milner, John. "Vince McMahon." *Slam! Wrestling*, February 5, 2005. Retrieved
    March 2009 (http://www.canoe.ca/Slam/Wrestling/Bios/
    mcmahon-vince.html).

Montgomery, James. "Chris Benoit Had Steroids, Other Drugs in His System
    at Time of Murder-Suicide." MTV, July 17, 2007. Retrieved November 15,
    2008 (http://www.mtv.com/news/articles/1564953/20070717/
    index.jhtml).

Muchnick, Irv. *Wrestling Babylon.* Toronto, Canada: ECW Press, 2007.

National Institute on Drug Abuse. "NIDA InfoFacts: Steroids (Anabolic-
    Androgenic)." National Institutes of Health. Retrieved January 2, 2008.
    (http://www.drugabuse.gov/Infofacts/steroids.html).

National Wrestling Coaches Association. "NATA Official Release on Steroids."
    March 24, 2008. Retrieved November 15, 2008 (http://www.nwcaonline.
    com/steroids.cfm).

New York Times. "Hulk Hogan on Witness Stand Tells of Steroid Use in
    Wrestling." July 15, 1994. Retrieved November 15, 2008 (http://query.
    nytimes.com/gst/fullpage.html?sec=health&res=9C0DE6D6103FF936A
    25754C0A962958260).

Quinn, T. J. "Top WWE Names Emerge in Doping Scandal." *New York Daily News*,
    August 30, 2007. Retrieved December 20, 2008 (http://www.nydailynews.
    com/sports/2007/08/30/2007-08-30_top_wwe_names_emerge_in_
    doping_scandal.html).

Sports Illustrated. "Fourteen Wrestlers Tied to Pipeline." August 30, 2007. Retrieved November 20, 2008 (http://sportsillustrated.cnn.com/2007/more/08/30/wrestlers/index.html).

Stehlin, Doris. "Physician Convicted in Steroid Distribution—George T. Zahorian III." *FDA Consumer*, November 1991. Retrieved November 20, 2008 (http://findarticles.com/p/articles/mi_m1370/is_n9_v25/ai_11621889).

Swartz, Jon. "High Death Rate Lingers Behind Fun Facade of Pro Wrestling." *USA Today*, March 12, 2004. Retrieved November 20, 2008 (http://www.usatoday.com/sports/2004-03-12-pro-wrestling_x.htm).

Wertheim, L. Jon, and David Epstein. "The Godfather." *Sports Illustrated*, March 11, 2008. Retrieved December 20, 2008 (http://sportsillustrated.cnn.com/2008/magazine/03/11/steroids.godfather).

WrestlingInc.com. "A New WWE Talent, # of Chavo Guerrero Suspensions, & More." April 6, 2008. Retrieved November 20, 2008 (http://www.wrestlinginc.com/news/2008/46/chavo_guerrero_321050.shtml).

Wrestling Steroids. "Professional Wrestlers and Anabolic Steroids." Retrieved December 20, 2008 (http://www.wrestlingsteroids.com).

WSBTV.com. "Lawyer: Benoit's Diary Shows Signs of Depression, Dementia." September 14, 2007. Retrieved November 12, 2008 (http://www.wsbtv.com/news/14109745/detail.html).

WSBTV.com. "Police Report: Chris Benoit Thought His Marriage Was Failing; Nancy Scared." February 12, 2008. Retrieved November 12, 2008 (http://www.wsbtv.com/news/15281734/detail.html).

INDEX

About the Author

Jeri Freedman has a B.A. from Harvard University. For fifteen years, she worked for companies in the medical field. She is the author of more than twenty-five young adult nonfiction books, many of them published by Rosen Publishing. Among her previous titles are *The Human Population and the Nitrogen Cycle*; *Hemophilia*; *Hepatitis B*; *Lymphoma: Current and Emerging Trends in Detection and Treatment*; *How Do We Know About Genetics and Heredity?*; *The Mental and Physical Effects of Obesity*; *Everything You Need to Know About Genetically Modified Foods*; *Autism*; *Applications and Limitations of Taxonomy in Classification of Organisms: An Anthology of Current Thought*; and *Drug Abuse and Society: Steroids*.

Photo Credits

Designer: Nicole Russo; Editor: Christopher Roberts;
Photo Researcher: Marty Levick